MW01230516

Sloth Practice

This Log Book Belongs To

_____

"A man who is master of patience is master of everything else."

Sir George Saville, English Politician 1726-1784

Congratulations!

Welcome to Sloth Practice!

You are about to unlock easy Brain Hacks to benefit you, whatever you want to learn!
I rely on them especially when I am preparing multiple productions at the same time.
Having a Clear Goal, Knowing What to Do, How many times to do it, and WHEN
are simple tricks with huge gains. Log it here and you can see for yourself!
We *should* all know that LISTENING is essential.
Did you know that the timing of SLEEP is a critical piece of the puzzle?
Our friendly Sloth shows us - a few deliberate minutes in the morning
and again in the evening gives greater results than one unfocused marathon session!

Leslie Brown Katz, violinist
Los Angeles Opera, Suzuki Teacher, and
Proud Mama of three graduate sloths!

"Your now isn't your always."
— Molly M. Cantrell-Kraig, *Circuit Train Your Brain: Daily Habits That Develop Resilience*

How To Use This Logbook

At the Lesson - Fill in your 3 Clear Practice Tasks, Practice Nuggets, and what your Teacher wants you to Focus On.

During the Week:
Log your Practice Dates in a Leaf corresponding to the Time of Day

3 Clear Practice Tasks

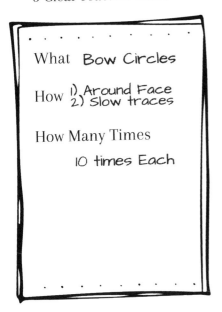

What   Bow Circles

How   1) Around Face
      2) Slow traces

How Many Times
      10 times Each

Focus Point Alert
for the Week

Thumbs!

Staff to write Practice Nuggets

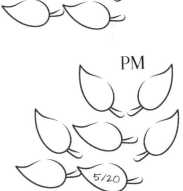

AM

5/21

PM

5/20

Questions for next Lesson?

Date _____

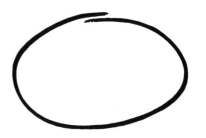

What

How

How Many Times

What

How

How Many Times

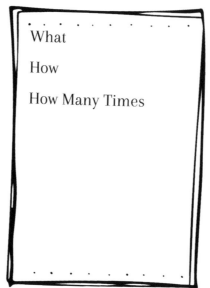

What

How

How Many Times

♫ LISTEN Like a Maniac!

_____

AM

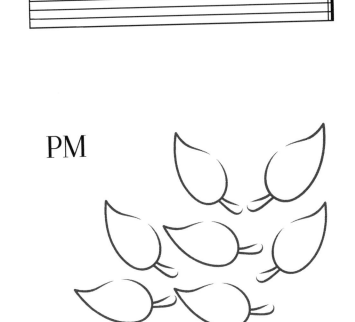

PM

Questions for next Lesson?

Date _____

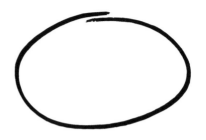

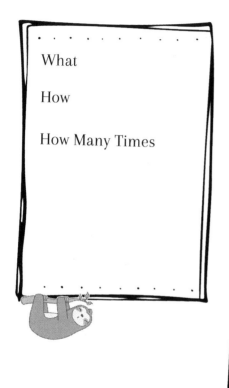

What

How

How Many Times

♪♫ LISTEN Like a Maniac!

What

How

How Many Times

What

How

How Many Times

AM

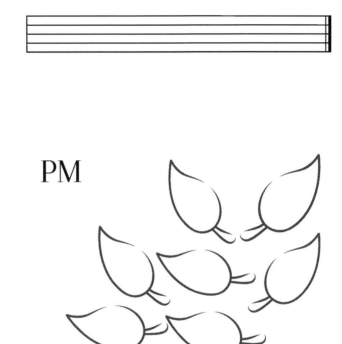

PM

Questions for next Lesson?

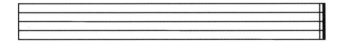

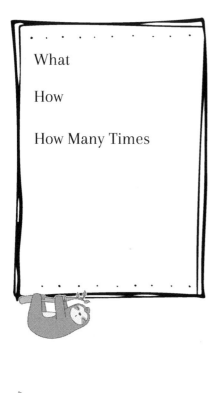

What

How

How Many Times

Date _____

What

How

How Many Times

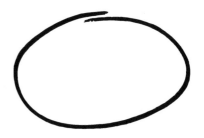

What

How

How Many Times

🎵 LISTEN Like a Maniac!

AM

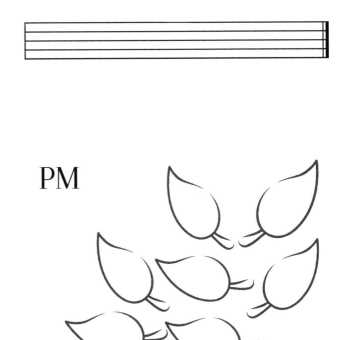

PM

Questions for next Lesson?

Date _____

What

How

How Many Times

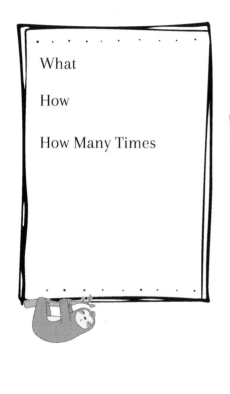

What

How

How Many Times

What

How

How Many Times

🎵 LISTEN Like a Maniac!

AM

PM

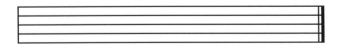

Questions for next Lesson?

Date _____

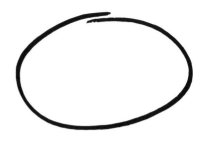

What

How

How Many Times

What

How

How Many Times

What

How

How Many Times

🎵🎵 LISTEN Like a Maniac!

AM

PM

Questions for next Lesson?

What

How

How Many Times

Date _____

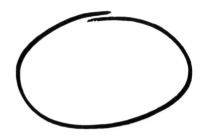

What

How

How Many Times

What

How

How Many Times

🎵 LISTEN Like a Maniac!

AM

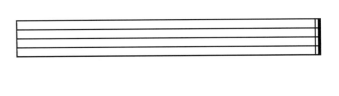

PM

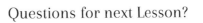

Questions for next Lesson?

What

How

How Many Times

Date _____

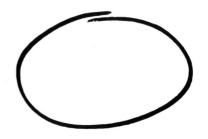

What

How

How Many Times

What

How

How Many Times

♫♪ LISTEN Like a Maniac!

AM

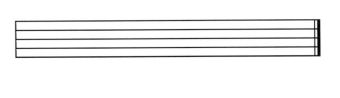

PM

Questions for next Lesson?

Date _____

What

How

How Many Times

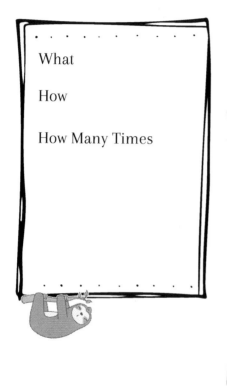

What

How

How Many Times

🎵 LISTEN Like a Maniac!

What

How

How Many Times

AM

PM

Questions for next Lesson?

Date _____

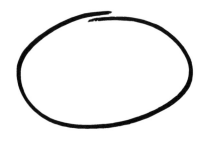

What

How

How Many Times

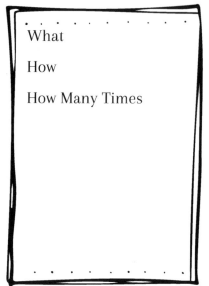

What

How

How Many Times

What

How

How Many Times

🎵 LISTEN Like a Maniac!

AM

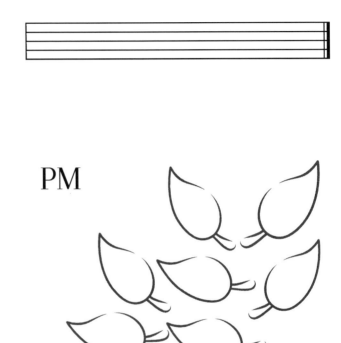

PM

Questions for next Lesson?

Date _____

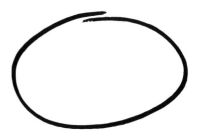

What

How

How Many Times

What

How

How Many Times

What

How

How Many Times

♫ LISTEN Like a Maniac!

AM

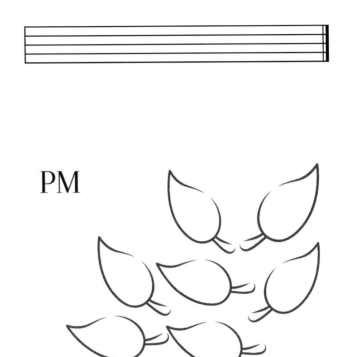

PM

Questions for next Lesson?

Date _____

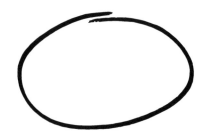

What

How

How Many Times

What

How

How Many Times

What

How

How Many Times

🎵 LISTEN Like a Maniac!

AM

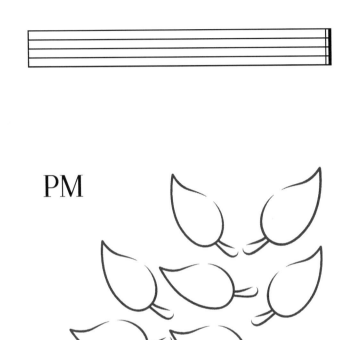

PM

Questions for next Lesson?

Date _____

What

How

How Many Times

What

How

How Many Times

What

How

How Many Times

🎵 LISTEN Like a Maniac!

AM

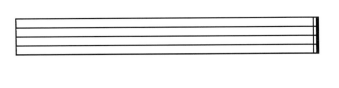

PM

Questions for next Lesson?

Date _____

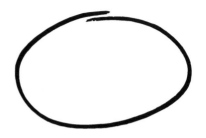

What

How

How Many Times

What

How

How Many Times

What

How

How Many Times

🎵 LISTEN Like a Maniac!

AM

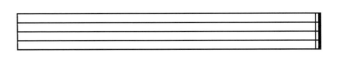

PM

Questions for next Lesson?

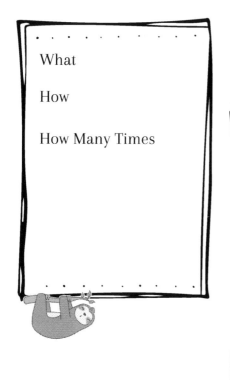

What

How

How Many Times

Date _____

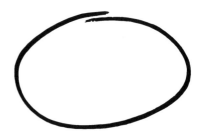

What

How

How Many Times

What

How

How Many Times

🎵 LISTEN Like a Maniac!

AM

PM

Questions for next Lesson?

Date _____

What

How

How Many Times

What

How

How Many Times

What

How

How Many Times

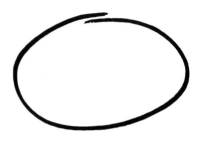

🎵 LISTEN Like a Maniac!

AM

PM

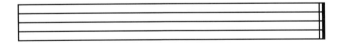

Questions for next Lesson?

Date _____

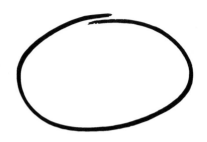

What

How

How Many Times

What

How

How Many Times

What

How

How Many Times

🎵 LISTEN Like a Maniac!

AM

PM

Questions for next Lesson?

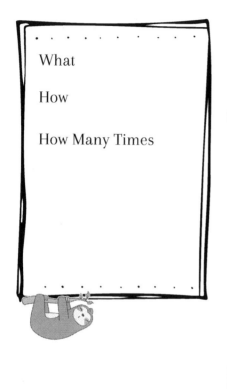

What

How

How Many Times

Date _____

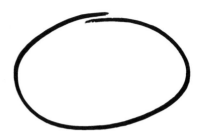

What

How

How Many Times

What

How

How Many Times

🎵 LISTEN Like a Maniac!

AM

PM

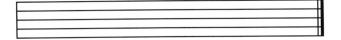

Questions for next Lesson?

Date _____

What

How

How Many Times

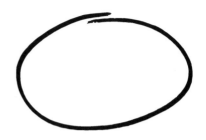

What

How

How Many Times

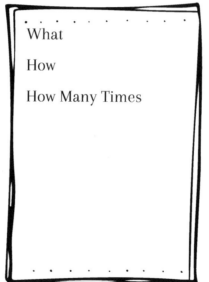

What

How

How Many Times

♫ LISTEN Like a Maniac!

AM

PM

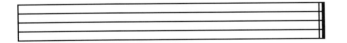

Questions for next Lesson?

Date _____

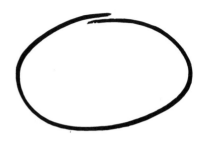

What

How

How Many Times

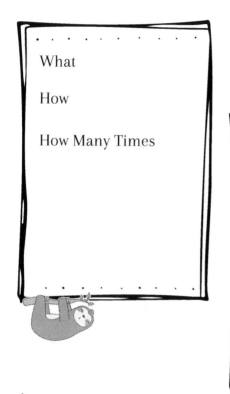

What

How

How Many Times

What

How

How Many Times

🎵 LISTEN Like a Maniac!

AM

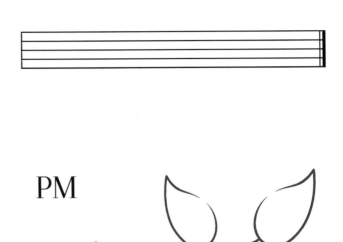

PM

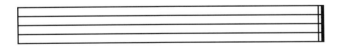

Questions for next Lesson?

Date _____

What

How

How Many Times

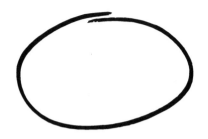

What

How

How Many Times

What

How

How Many Times

🎵 LISTEN Like a Maniac!

AM

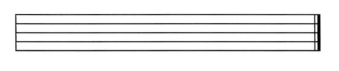

PM

Questions for next Lesson?

What

How

How Many Times

Date _____

What

How

How Many Times

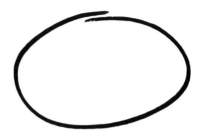

What

How

How Many Times

🎵 LISTEN Like a Maniac!

AM

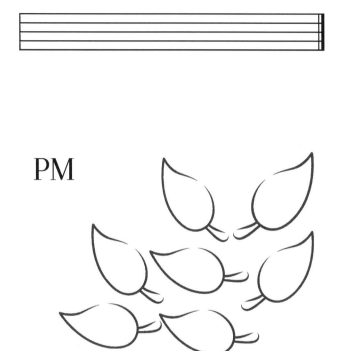

PM

Questions for next Lesson?

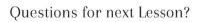

Date _____

What

How

How Many Times

What

How

How Many Times

What

How

How Many Times

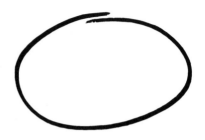

♫ LISTEN Like a Maniac!

AM

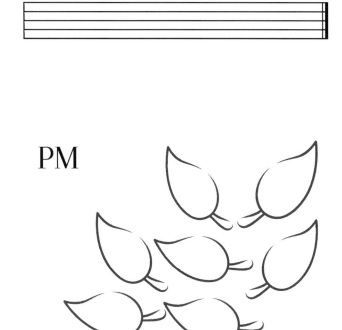

PM

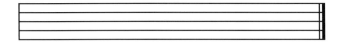

Questions for next Lesson?

Date _____

What

How

How Many Times

What

How

How Many Times

What

How

How Many Times

♫ LISTEN Like a Maniac!

AM

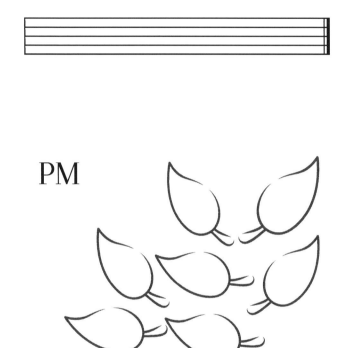

PM

Questions for next Lesson?

Date _____

What

How

How Many Times

What

How

How Many Times

What

How

How Many Times

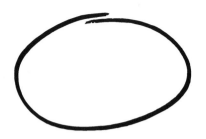 LISTEN Like a Maniac!

AM

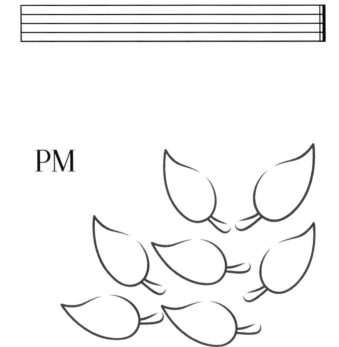

PM

Questions for next Lesson?

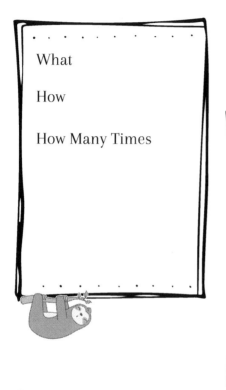

What

How

How Many Times

Date _____

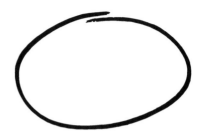

What

How

How Many Times

What

How

How Many Times

🎵🎶 LISTEN Like a Maniac!

AM

PM

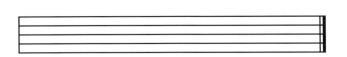

Questions for next Lesson?

Date _____

What

How

How Many Times

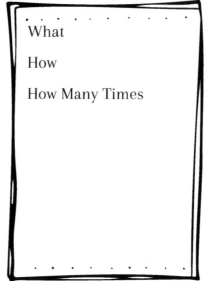

What

How

How Many Times

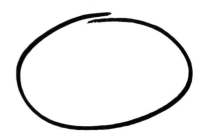

What

How

How Many Times

🎵 LISTEN Like a Maniac!

AM

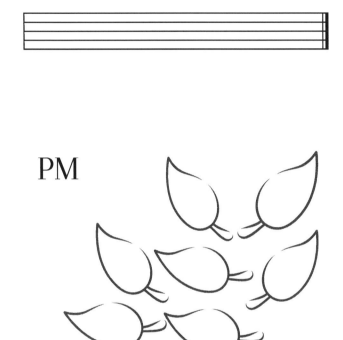

PM

Questions for next Lesson?

Date _____

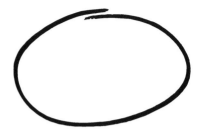

What

How

How Many Times

What

How

How Many Times

What

How

How Many Times

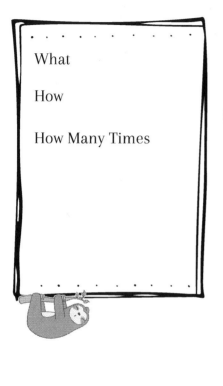

🎵 LISTEN Like a Maniac!

AM

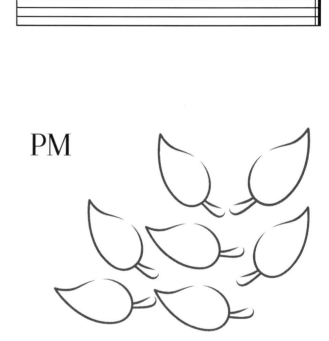

PM

Questions for next Lesson?

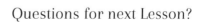

Date _____

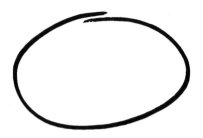

What

How

How Many Times

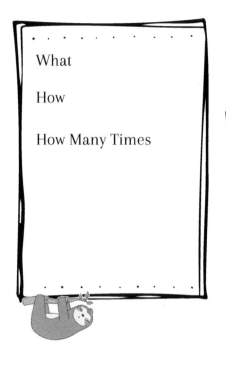

What

How

How Many Times

What

How

How Many Times

What

How

How Many Times

🎵🎶 LISTEN Like a Maniac!

AM

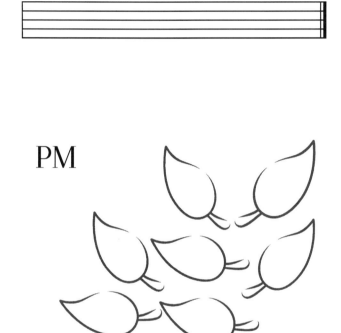

PM

Questions for next Lesson?

Date _____

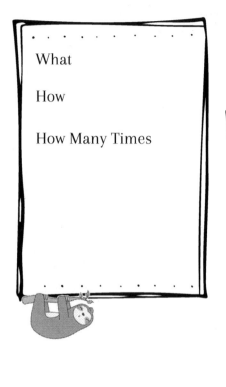

What

How

How Many Times

🎵 LISTEN Like a Maniac!

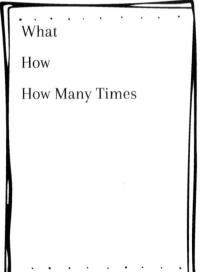

What

How

How Many Times

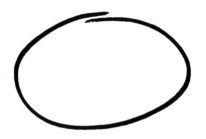

What

How

How Many Times

AM

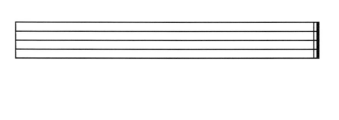

PM

Questions for next Lesson?

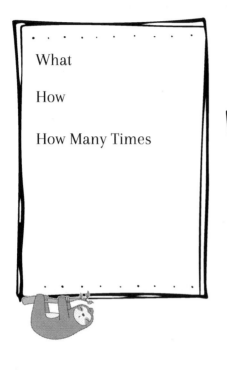

What

How

How Many Times

Date _____

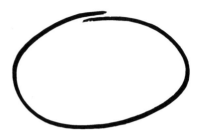

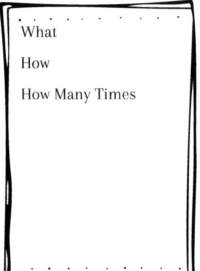

What

How

How Many Times

What

How

How Many Times

🎵🎶 LISTEN Like a Maniac!

AM

PM

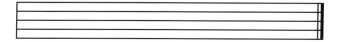

Questions for next Lesson?

Date _____

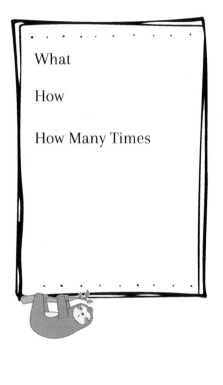

What

How

How Many Times

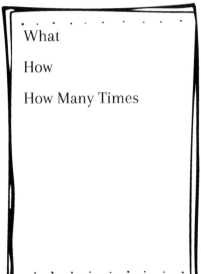

What

How

How Many Times

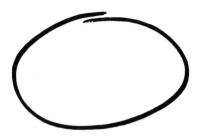

What

How

How Many Times

LISTEN Like a Maniac!

AM

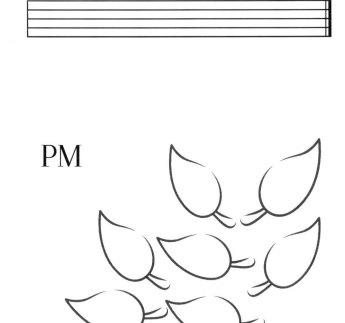

PM

Questions for next Lesson?

Date _____

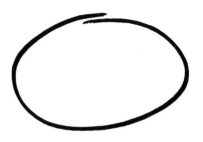

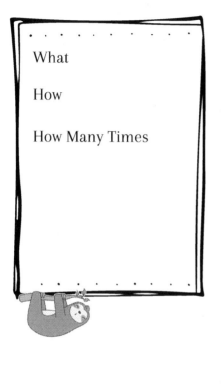

What

How

How Many Times

What

How

How Many Times

What

How

How Many Times

🎵🎶 LISTEN Like a Maniac!

AM

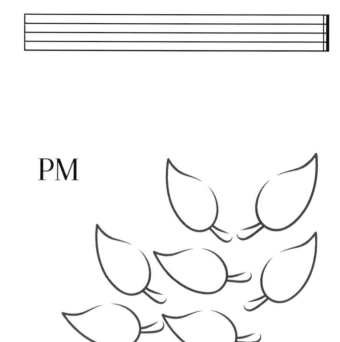

PM

Questions for next Lesson?

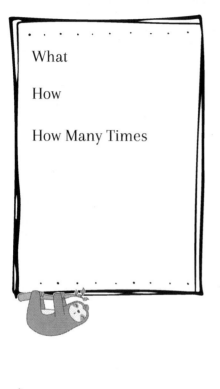

What

How

How Many Times

🎵 LISTEN Like a Maniac!

Date _____

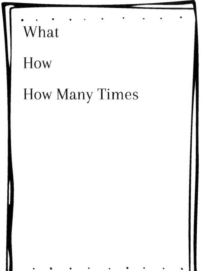

What

How

How Many Times

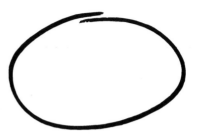

What

How

How Many Times

AM

PM

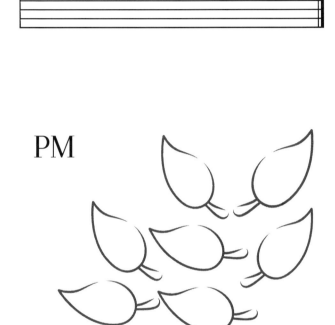

Questions for next Lesson?

Date _____

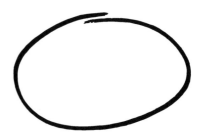

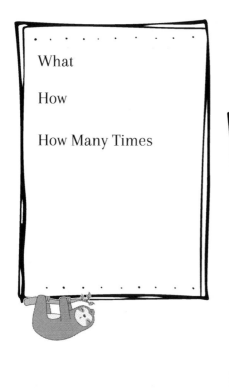

What

How

How Many Times

What

How

How Many Times

What

How

How Many Times

🎵 LISTEN Like a Maniac!

AM

PM

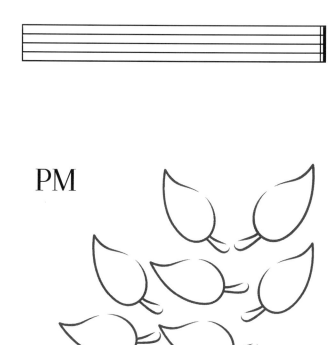

Questions for next Lesson?

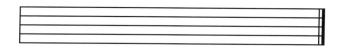

Date _____

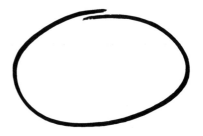

What

How

How Many Times

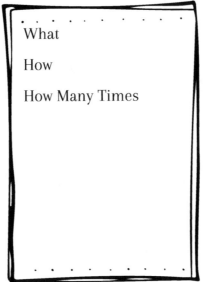

What

How

How Many Times

What

How

How Many Times

🎵 LISTEN Like a Maniac!

AM

PM

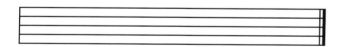

Questions for next Lesson?

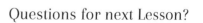

Date _____

What

How

How Many Times

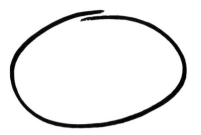

What

How

How Many Times

What

How

How Many Times

What

How

How Many Times

🎵 LISTEN Like a Maniac!

AM

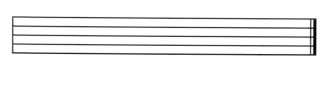

PM

Questions for next Lesson?

Date _____

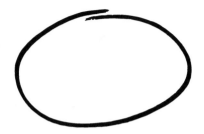

What

How

How Many Times

What

How

How Many Times

What

How

How Many Times

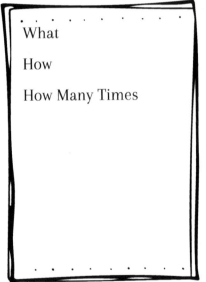

♫ LISTEN Like a Maniac!

_____

AM

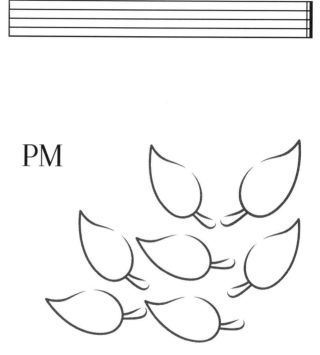

PM

Questions for next Lesson?

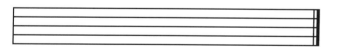

Date _____

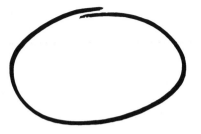

What

How

How Many Times

What

How

How Many Times

What

How

How Many Times

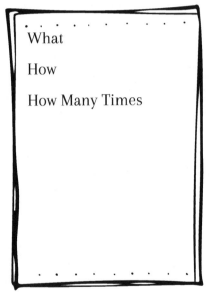

🎵 LISTEN Like a Maniac!

AM

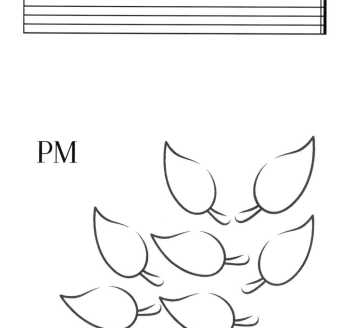

PM

Questions for next Lesson?

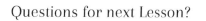

Date _____

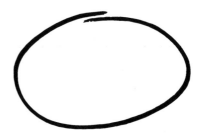

What

How

How Many Times

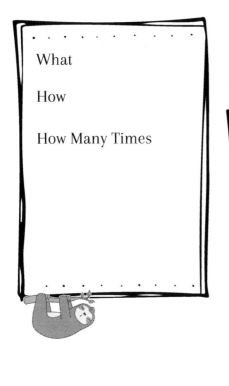

What

How

How Many Times

What

How

How Many Times

🎵 LISTEN Like a Maniac!

AM

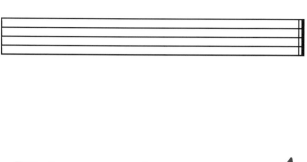

PM

Questions for next Lesson?

Date _____

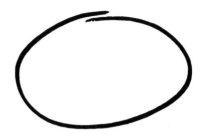

What

How

How Many Times

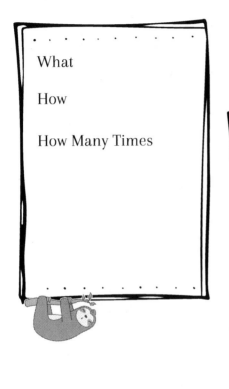

What

How

How Many Times

What

How

How Many Times

🎵🎶 LISTEN Like a Maniac!

AM

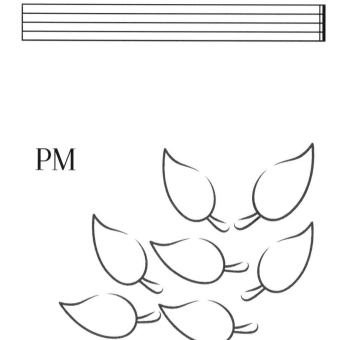

PM

Questions for next Lesson?

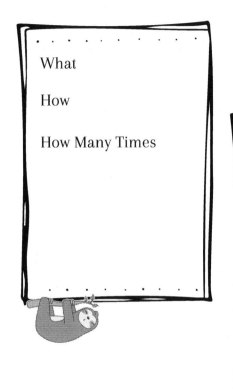

What

How

How Many Times

Date _____

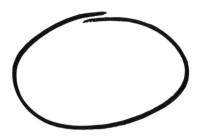

What

How

How Many Times

What

How

How Many Times

🎵 LISTEN Like a Maniac!

AM

PM

Questions for next Lesson?

Date _____

What

How

How Many Times

What

How

How Many Times

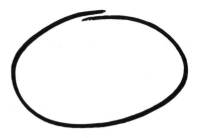

What

How

How Many Times

🎵 LISTEN Like a Maniac!

AM

PM

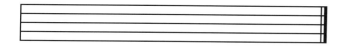

Questions for next Lesson?

Date _____

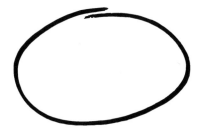

What

How

How Many Times

What

How

How Many Times

What

How

How Many Times

🎵 LISTEN Like a Maniac!

AM

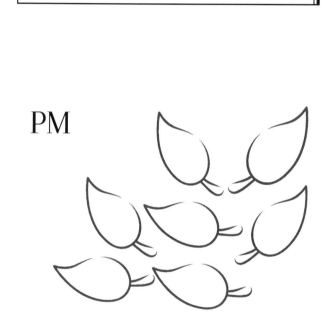

PM

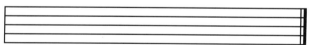

Questions for next Lesson?

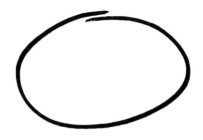

Date _____

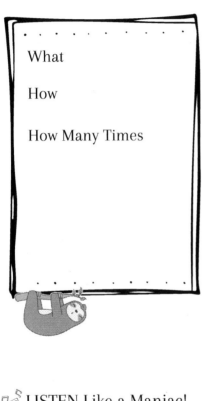

What

How

How Many Times

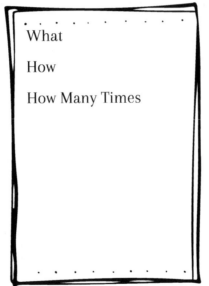

What

How

How Many Times

What

How

How Many Times

🎵 LISTEN Like a Maniac!

AM

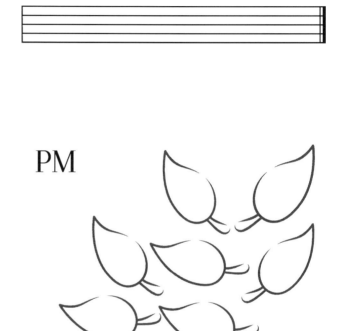

PM

Questions for next Lesson?

Date _____

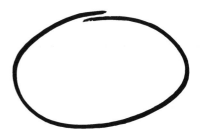

What

How

How Many Times

What

How

How Many Times

What

How

How Many Times

♫♪ LISTEN Like a Maniac!

AM

PM

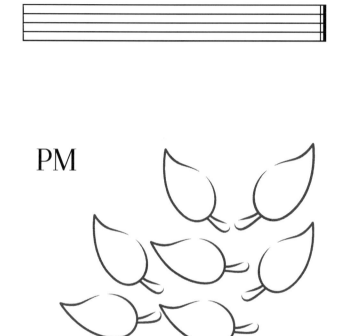

Questions for next Lesson?

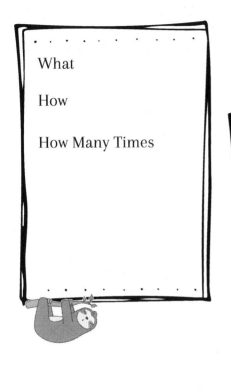

What

How

How Many Times

Date _____

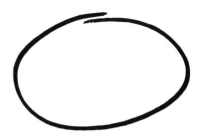

What

How

How Many Times

🎵🎶 LISTEN Like a Maniac!

What

How

How Many Times

AM

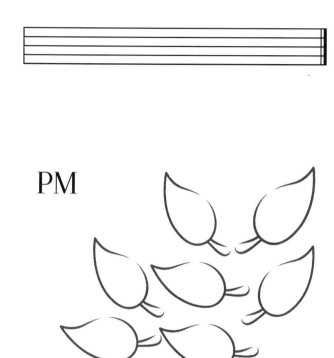

PM

Questions for next Lesson?

Date _____

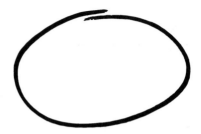

What

How

How Many Times

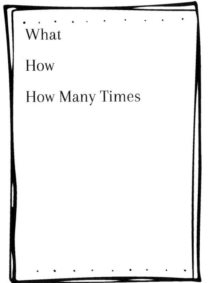

What

How

How Many Times

What

How

How Many Times

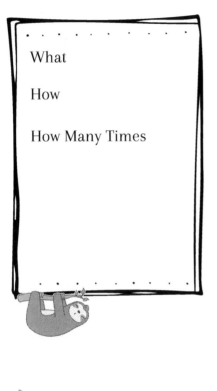

🎵🎵 LISTEN Like a Maniac!

AM

PM

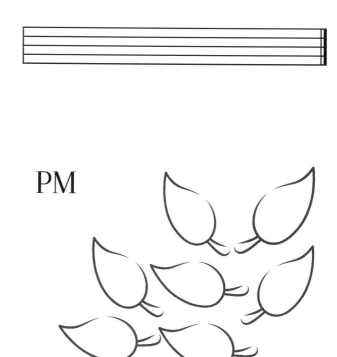

Questions for next Lesson?

Date _____

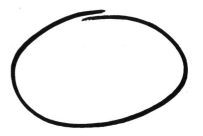

What

How

How Many Times

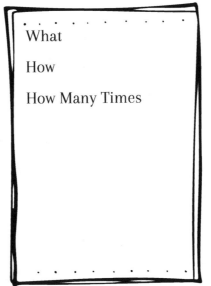

What

How

How Many Times

What

How

How Many Times

🎵 LISTEN Like a Maniac!

AM

PM

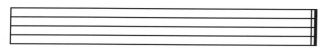

Questions for next Lesson?

Date _____

What

How

How Many Times

What

How

How Many Times

What

How

How Many Times

🎵 LISTEN Like a Maniac!

AM

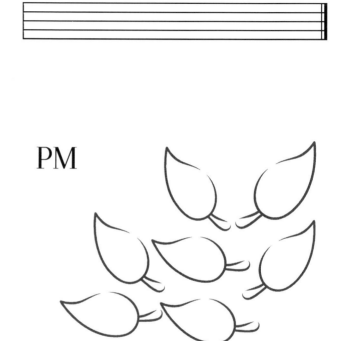

PM

Questions for next Lesson?

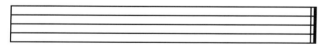

Date _____

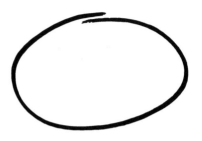

What

How

How Many Times

What

How

How Many Times

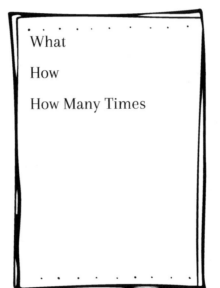

What

How

How Many Times

🎵 LISTEN Like a Maniac!

AM

PM

Questions for next Lesson?

Date _____

What

How

How Many Times

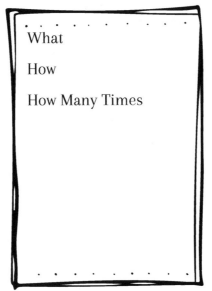

What

How

How Many Times

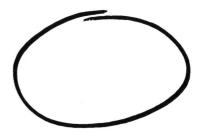

What

How

How Many Times

🎵 LISTEN Like a Maniac!

AM

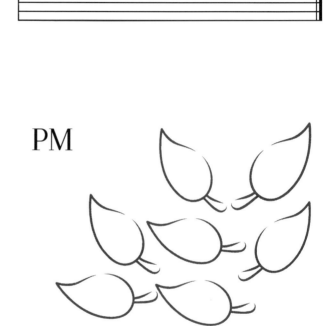

PM

Questions for next Lesson?

Date _____

What

How

How Many Times

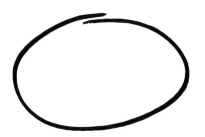

What

How

How Many Times

What

How

How Many Times

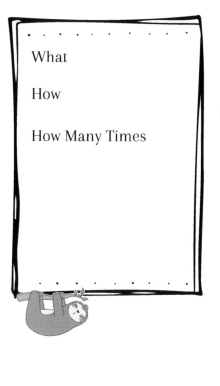

♫♪ LISTEN Like a Maniac!

AM

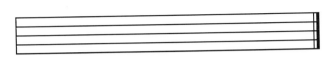

PM

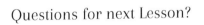

Questions for next Lesson?

My Wish List

WRITE YOUR GOALS HERE
THEY CAN BE PIECES THAT YOU WANT TO PLAY OR SKILLS TO PERFECT,
CHECK BACK HERE EVERY ONCE IN A WHILE
TO SEE HOW CLOSE YOU ARE GETTING!

My Aha Moments

Ready for Recital

LIST YOUR POLISHED PIECES HERE -
IF SOMEONE SAYS "PLAY SOMETHING" AND YOUR MIND GOES BLANK,
YOU CAN JUST FLIP OPEN THIS PAGE AND HAVE A LOOK!

Made in the USA
Columbia, SC
25 June 2023

19164401R00061